CONCERTO in F
For PIANO and ORCHESTRA

Two Copies Necessary for Performance

GEORGE GERSHWIN®

F O R E W O R D

George Gershwin was born in Brooklyn, N. Y., September 1898 and died in Hollywood, July 1937.

Gershwin came to us from the very soil of our great American melting pot. He was intimately acquainted with the grind of life; its perpetual struggle, its joys, its sorrows and its aspirations. He knew his fellow man, was sensitive to his reactions, his likes and dislikes, and as a creative genius was able eloquently to portray in music "the blood and feeling of the American people".

His idiom was the idiom of the day; call it "jazz" or what you will, it was nevertheless a musical expression of a great people. Frowned upon by the musically intelligent as tawdry, cheap and unmusical, yet Gershwin chose the idiom of the people to express himself musically. True, others had done the same, but the tunes of Gershwin were in some way "different". When they were exuberant, they seemed to outstrip all other contemporary attempts at exuberance; and when they were expressive, tender or melancholy, they knew no equal. But something else had crept into the music, something that made itself felt immediately to performer or listener alike. Gershwin had something to say musically, even through the confinements and limitations of the popular song form. Above all, Gershwin *wanted* to say something.

The test came at that memorable concert by Paul Whiteman and his orchestra in a program of "symphonic jazz" at Aeolian Hall February 12th, 1924. Gershwin had written for the occasion his *Rhapsody in Blue*. It became the corner-stone of American musical expression. In it, the serious musician found that the "breach" between the music of the masses, the music of Tin Pan Alley and that of more cultivated taste was actually non-existent. There was music of questionable worth in the classic libraries as well as there was worthless music from the region of Tin Pan Alley — and after all, was it not the people themselves who became both judge and jury in either case?

Following the *Rhapsody in Blue* and its instantaneous success, Walter Damrosch, conductor of the New York Symphony Society, commissioned Gershwin to write a Concerto for piano and orchestra. It was a supreme test, but the CONCERTO IN F resulted and was performed for the first time with Gershwin as soloist under Damrosch with the New York Symphony Orchestra at Carnegie Hall December 3, 1925.

In the opinion of this chronicler, it is his greatest work. Gershwin, for the first time in his life, came to grips with a severe musical form, a form known to the masters and assiduously avoided by many of them. He was confronted with the problems of symphonic orchestration and instrumental balance *per se* and with the solo piano. He was obliged to bring to this formidable structure a musical idiom hitherto never attempted— and he succeeded on all accounts, resulting in a work which today, after repeated hearings, has lost none of its greatness, freshness or brilliance.

Possibly, when those inescapable qualities in Gershwin's music, in the just evaluation which time brings to all things, are truly understood and appreciated, and sound an echo throughout the world, he will have reached his real stature among musicians.

F. Campbell-Watson

Concerto in F
For Piano And Orchestra ✶

I

GEORGE GERSHWIN

✶ *Small notes in 1st Pianoforte contain additional orchestral notes not practicable for II Pianoforte alone.*

C I

C I

22

C I

26

C I

II

Adagio

Andante con moto

Solo Trumpet (muted with felt crown)

Piano I

Piano II

36

C II

38

C II

C II

46

III

Allegro agitato

Listesso tempo

Piano II

c III

Listesso tempo

56

C III

C III

58

C III

60

C III